“The Only Thing Necessary for the Triumph of Evil is for Good Men to Do Nothing"

"Political Quotes by Influential Leaders"

Book by

B.J. Wilsey

Quotes included in this book are sourced from public speeches, writings, and historical records of the following individuals:
Franklin Delano Roosevelt
John F. Kennedy
Sir Winston Leonard Spencer Churchill
Abraham Lincoln
Martin Luther King Jr. Nelson Mandela Mahatma Gandhi Albert Einstein
George Orwell
John Emerich Edward Dalberg-Acton, 1st Baron Acton
Every effort has been made to obtain proper permissions for the use of these quotes. If any copyright or attribution issues arise, please contact the publisher.
Cover design by B.J. Wilsey
Interior layout and design by B.J. Wilsey
2nd Edition: 2024

Acknowledgments

The only thing Necessary for the

Triumph of evil is for good men to

Do nothing"

This quote is attributed to

Edmund Burke

DISCLAIMER

The content of this book, "political quotes by influential leaders," is provided for educational and informational purposes only. The quotes included in this book are sourced from public speeches, writings, and historical records of the following individuals: franklin Delano Roosevelt, john f. Kennedy, Sir Winston Leonard spencer Churchill, Abraham Lincoln, martin Luther king jr., nelson Mandela, mahatma Gandhi, albert einstein, George Orwell, and john Emerich Edward Dalberg Acton, 1st baron Acton.

Accuracy of quotes

Every effort has been made to ensure the accuracy and authenticity of the quotes presented in this book. However, it is important to note that historical records and interpretations may vary. Quotes may have been paraphrased, translated, or taken out of context over time. Readers are encouraged to verify quotes independently and consult primary sources for the most accurate representation of the individuals' words and beliefs.

No endorsement or affiliation

This book is not affiliated with any political party, organization, or ideology. The inclusion of quotes from these historical figures does not imply an endorsement of any viewpoint or agenda. The intent is solely to provide insight into the thoughts and perspectives of these influential leaders.

COPYRIGHT AND FAIR USE

The quotes included in this book are presented under the principles of fair use and in compliance with applicable copyright laws. Efforts have been made to respect copyright and provide proper attribution where necessary. If you believe that any content in this book violates copyright or attribution guidelines, please contact the publisher.

Author's note

The author of this book has endeavored to present a diverse and balanced selection of quotes from the mentioned political leaders. The author's interpretations, if any, are solely their own and do not reflect the views or intentions of the individuals quoted.

Reader responsibility

Readers are encouraged to engage critically with the content of this book and to consider the historical context, evolving perspectives, and complexity of the issues discussed. It is essential to approach.

these quotes with an open mind and a commitment to understanding the broader context in which they were made.

Disclaimer changes

The publisher reserves the right to update and amend this disclaimer as necessary to reflect changes in the book's content, legal requirements, or other relevant considerations.

About the Author

B.J. Wilsey is a highly accomplished retired Senior Air Force NCO, businessman, and veteran of numerous overseas and domestic deployments. During his distinguished military career, he was stationed in several overseas, including Japan, France, Spain, Alaska and Australia.

Following his retirement from the Air Force, B.J. and his family ventured into entrepreneurship and successfully ran their business for over 20 years before retiring once again.

B.J. Wilsey holds Associate of Applied Science Degrees in Material Management and Resource Management, a testament to his commitment to lifelong learning and professional development.

He continues to remain active in his community and supports various veteran causes.

B.J. Wilsey

CONTENTS

Chapter 1
Franklin Delano Roosevelt

Franklin Delano Roosevelt (January 30, 1882 — April 12, 1945), Commonly known by his initials FDR, was an American politician who served as the 32nd president of the United States from 1933 until his death in 1945. He directed the federal government during most of the Great Depression, implementing the New Deal in response to the most significant economic crisis in American history. He also built the New Deal coalition, realigning American politics into the Fifth Party System and defining American liberalism throughout the middle third of the 20th century. He was a member of the Democratic Party and is the only U.S.

president to have served more than eight years in office; his third and fourth terms were dominated by World War II.

"The only thing we have to fear is fear itself. "

This quote is attributed to Franklin D Roosevelt, the 32nd President of the United States, and was first used in his inaugural address on March 4, 1933. The quote is often interpreted as a call to action against fear and anxiety, which can be paralyzing and prevent people from acting. Roosevelt's speech was delivered during the Great Depression, a time of great economic hardship and uncertainty in the United States. The quote has since become one of the most famous presidential quotes in American history and is often used to encourage people to face their fears and overcome adversity. of the United States from 1933 until his death in 1945. He directed the federal government during most of the Great Depression, implementing the New Deal in response to the most significant economic crisis in American history. He also built the New Deal coalition, realigning American politics into the Fifth Party System and defining American liberalism throughout the middle third of the 20th century. He was a member of the Democratic Party and is the only U.S. president to have served more than eight years in office; his third and fourth terms were dominated by World War II.

"The test of our progress is not whether we add more to the abundance of those who have much; it is whether we provide enough for those who have too little.

Franklin D. Roosevelt encapsulates a fundamental principle of social justice and equitable progress. Roosevelt was a key figure in American history, particularly during the Great Depression and World War II, and his policies often centered on addressing economic inequality and providing support for those in need.

"In politics, nothing happens by accident. If it happens, you can bet it was planned that way. "

This statement reflects the idea that political events and developments are often the result of deliberate actions, strategies, and planning, rather than random occurrences. Roosevelt's presidency, particularly during his time in office from 1933 to 1945, saw the United States navigate significant challenges, including the Great Depression and World War II. His leadership style was marked by careful planning and deliberate policy initiatives to address these crises. This quote aligns with his approach to governance, suggesting that many political outcomes are the result of calculated decisions and actions taken by leaders and their administrations.

"The only sure bulwark of continuing liberty is a government strong enough to protect the interests of the people, and a people strong enough and well enough informed to maintain its sovereign control over the government. "

This quote emphasizes the importance of a strong and informed government and an engaged and informed citizenry as essential elements for the preservation of liberty.

Government Strength: Roosevelt suggests that a government needs to be strong enough to protect the interests of its people. This implies that a government should have the power and authority to enforce laws, maintain order, and defend the rights and welfare of its citizens. Without a strong government, there may be a power vacuum or instability that could threaten individual liberties.

Informed Citizens: The quote also underscores the significance of an informed citizenry. For democracy to function effectively, citizens need to be well-informed about political issues, policies, and the actions of their government. Informed citizens are better equipped to make educated decisions when participating in the democratic process, such as voting and engaging in political discourse.

Sovereign Control: Roosevelt mentions "sovereign control over the government, " which reflects the idea that in a democratic system, the ultimate authority resides with the people. Citizens should have the ability to hold their government accountable and influence its actions through democratic processes like elections, petitioning, and advocacy.

In essence, Roosevelt's quote underscores the interdependence of a strong government and an informed and engaged citizenry in maintaining and preserving liberty. It suggests that a balance must be struck between the government's capacity to protect the rights and interests of the people and the people's capacity to actively participate in and influence the government's decisions. This balance is seen as crucial for the continuation of liberty within a democratic system.

"We are all in this together, and we are going to solve our problems together. "

"We are all in this together, and we are going to solve our problems together." This statement emphasizes the importance of unity and collaboration in addressing challenges and finding solutions. It reflects the idea that when individuals, communities, or even nations work together towards a common goal, they are more likely to overcome obstacles and achieve success. This sentiment is often invoked in times of crisis or when facing complex issues that require collective effort and solidarity.

"Democracy cannot succeed unless those who express their choice are prepared to choose wisely. The real safeguard of democracy, therefore, is education. "

The statement, "Democracy cannot succeed unless those who express their choice are prepared to choose wisely. The real safeguard of democracy, therefore, is education," highlights the fundamental importance of education in a democratic society. Here's a breakdown of its key points:

Choosing Wisely: The statement suggests that the success of a democratic system depends on the informed and thoughtful choices made by its citizens. In a democracy, individuals have the right to vote and express their preferences through elections, but the effectiveness of this process relies on people making well-informed decisions rather than uninformed or impulsive choices.

Safeguard of Democracy: The phrase "real safeguard of democracy" implies that while there may be various mechanisms and institutions in place to protect democratic principles, the most significant and reliable safeguard is education. In other words, an educated and informed populace is crucial for the long-term stability and health of a democratic society.

Education 's Role: Education is portrayed as how citizens acquire the knowledge, critical thinking skills, and information necessary to make informed decisions. It provides individuals with the tools to understand complex issues, evaluate candidates and policies, and engage in civic participation effectively. In summary, this statement underscores the vital role of education in maintaining and strengthening a democratic society. It suggests that a well-informed and educated citizenry is essential for the proper functioning of democracy, as it enables people to make thoughtful and responsible choices in the political process.

"Men and nature must work hand in hand. The throwing out of balance of the resources of nature throws out of balance also the lives of men. "

In a message to Congress on the use of our national resources on January 24, 1935. FDR was addressing the problems of environmental degradation and social inequality that resulted from the exploitation of natural resources by previous generations. He advocated for a more balanced and sustainable approach to managing the land, water, and minerals of the nation, as well as the occupations and living conditions of the people. He also emphasized the importance of planning and cooperation among the various agencies of the federal government to achieve this goal.

"The liberty of a democracy is not safe if the people tolerate the growth of private power to a point where it becomes stronger than their democratic state itself. "

He was warning about the dangers of fascism and the concentration of economic power in the hands of a few corporations. He argued that democracy requires a balance between private enterprise and public interest, and that the government should intervene to prevent the abuse of monopoly power. He also linked the economic crisis of the Great Depression to the failure of the business system to provide employment and a decent standard of living for the people.

"Let us never forget that government is ourselves and not an alien power over us. The ultimate rulers of our democracy are not a President and senators and congressmen and government officials, but the voters of this country, "

He said these words in a speech on July 8, 1938, at Marietta, Ohio, where he dedicated a monument to the pioneers who settled Northwest Territory. He emphasized the importance of democracy and the role of the people in shaping their own government. The quote has been widely cited and used by various politicians, activists, and writers to inspire civic engagement and political participation.

"More than an end to war, we want an end to the beginnings of all wars. "

He wrote it in an undelivered address prepared for Jefferson Day, which was supposed to be on April 13, 1945. Unfortunately, he died on April 12, 1945, before he could deliver the speech. He was expressing his vision of peace after the Second World War, which was still raging in Europe and Asia. He wanted to end not only the current war, but also the causes of war, such as fear, hatred, ignorance, and greed. He believed that the United States had a great responsibility to lead the world toward a more just and peaceful order. He was also a great admirer of Thomas Jefferson, one of the founding fathers of the United States and a champion of democracy. He quoted Jefferson several times in his speech and praised his scientific and diplomatic achievements. You can read the full text of his speech herein. It is a remarkable document that shows his wisdom and *courage in a time of crisis.*

"Happiness is not in the mere possession of money; it lies in the joy of achievement, in the thrill of creative effort.

That is a very inspiring quote. It is attributed to Franklin D. Roosevelt, the 32nd president of the United States, who said it in his first inaugural address on March 4, 1933. He was trying to reassure the American people during the Great Depression, when many people were suffering from poverty and unemployment. He wanted to encourage them to work hard and pursue their dreams, rather than being afraid or greedy. He also criticized the practices of the "money changers" who had caused the economic crisis by their selfishness and incompetence.

The quote is like another one by Theodore Roosevelt, the 26th president of the United States and a distant cousin of Franklin D. Roosevelt. He said, "Happiness lies not in the mere possession of money; it lies in the joy of achievement, in the thrill of creative effort. The joy and moral stimulation of work must no longer be forgotten in the mad chase of evanescent profits." He expressed this idea in his book The New Nationalism, published in 1910, where he advocated for a more progressive and democratic society.

Both quotes suggest that happiness is not something that can be bought or measured by material wealth, but rather something that comes from within, from the satisfaction of doing something meaningful and valuable. They also imply that money is not an end, but a means to an end, and that it should be used wisely and responsibly, not wastefully or greedily. They also reflect the values and beliefs of the two presidents, who were both reformers and leaders who faced many challenges and difficulties in their times.

Chapter 2

President John F. Kennedy

President John F. Kennedy. Elected in 1960 as the 35th president of the United States, 43-year-old John F. Kennedy became one of the youngest U.S. presidents, as well as the first Roman Catholic to hold the office. Born into one of America's wealthiest families, he parlayed an elite education and a reputation as a military hero into a successful run for Congress in 1946 and for the Senate in 1952.

As president, Kennedy confronted mounting Cold War tensions in Cuba, Vietnam and elsewhere. He also led a renewed drive for public service and eventually provided federal support for the growing civil rights movement. His assassination on November 22, 1963, in Dallas,

Texas, sent shockwaves around the world and turned the all-too-human Kennedy into a larger-than-life heroic figure. To this day, historians continue to rank him among the best-loved presidents in American history.

"I do not believe that any of us would exchange places with any other people or any other generation. "

This is a famous quote from President John Kennedy's inaugural address on January 20, 1961. He was expressing his confidence and optimism in the American people and their role in defending freedom around the world. He also challenged them to participate in public service and contribute to the common good. He said this quote after declaring that he did not shrink from the responsibility of leading the nation in a time of great peril and opportunity. He wanted to inspire his fellow citizens to be proud of their heritage and their destiny.

"Ask not what your country can do for you; ask what you can do for your country"!

He said it during his inaugural address on January 20, 1961, as a way of inspiring Americans to be more active and patriotic citizens. The quote is often considered one of the best examples of rhetorical devices in speechwriting, such as antithesis, parallelism, and chiasmus. The quote also has a long history of being influenced by and influencing other similar expressions, such as those by Oliver Wendell Holmes, Charles de Gaulle, and Martin Luther King Jr. The quote is still relevant today, as it reminds us of the importance of civic engagement and public service for the common good.

"Change is the law of life. And those who look only to the past or present are certain to miss the future. " - From a speech in Frankfurt, Germany, on June 25, 1963.

He said this in a speech at the Paulskirche in Frankfurt, Germany, on June 25, 1963, during his visit to West Germany. The speech was about the challenges and opportunities of the Cold War, and the need for cooperation and innovation among the free nations. He also said: "For time and the world do not stand still. Change is the law of life. And those who look only to the past or present are certain to miss the future."

The quote reflects Kennedy's vision of progress and leadership, as well as his recognition of the rapid changes in the world. He believed that people should not be afraid of change but embrace it and use it to create a better future. He also encouraged people to look beyond their own interests and work together for the common good. He applied this philosophy to his domestic and foreign policies, such as the New Frontier, the Peace Corps, the Alliance for Progress, and the space program.

The quote is still relevant today, as we face new challenges and opportunities in the 21st century. It reminds us that change is inevitable and constant, and that we should be prepared and adaptable to it. It also inspires us to be proactive and creative in shaping our future, and to cooperate with others who share our values and goals.

"Our problems are man-made; therefore, they may be solved by man. And man can be as big as he wants. No problem of human destiny is beyond human beings. "

From a speech at the American University in Washington, D.C., on June 10, 1963, discussing the Cold War and nuclear disarmament. He said these words in his commencement address at American.

University in Washington, D.C., on June 10, 19631. He was talking about the need for peace and cooperation among nations, especially in the context of the Cold War and the nuclear arms race. He expressed his optimism that human beings can overcome their challenges and create a better world.

"Let us never negotiate out of fear. But let us never fear to negotiate. "

" But let us never fear negotiating. Inaugural Address, January 20, 1961.

"So let us begin anew remembering on both sides that civility is not a sign of weakness, and sincerity is always subject to proof. Let both sides explore what problems unite us instead of belaboring those problems which divide us. Let both sides, for the first time, formulate serious and precise proposals for the inspection and control of arms—and bring the absolute power to destroy other nations under the absolute control of all nations.

Prior to the initiation of the US-USSR negotiations on the draft agreement, I would like to have prepared for my approval a statement of objectives to be sought and the general principles to be followed in the negotiations. Such a statement would serve as a guide to the negotiators in responding to the Soviet counter proposals, as well as ensure that the negotiations are closely linked to our overall relations with the USSR. [National Security Action

Memorandum on the US USSR Commercial Air Transportation Agreement, March 21, 1961.

"The United States, as the world knows, will never start a war. We do not want a war. We do not now expect a war, this generation of Americans has already had enough—more than enough—of war and hate and oppression"

. We shall be prepared if others wish it. We shall be alerted to try to stop it. But we shall also do our part to build a world of peace where the weak are safe and the strong are just. We are not helpless before that task or hopeless of its success. Confident and unafraid, we labor on—not toward a strategy of annihilation but toward a strategy of peace. [American University Commencement

Address, June 10, 1963.]

"We cannot negotiate with people who say what's mine is mine and what's yours is negotiable. [News Conference, July 20, 1961.]

"The goal of education is the advancement of knowledge and the dissemination of truth. "

This is a famous quote by John F. Kennedy, the 35th president of the United States. He said this in a speech at Vanderbilt University on May 18, 1963. He emphasized the importance of education for the progress of society and the pursuit of truth. He believed that education should not only teach facts, but also values and ethics. He also encouraged students to be curious, creative, and critical thinkers, who can challenge the status quo and seek new solutions. He said, "The educated citizen has an obligation to serve the public. He may be a precinct worker or President. He may show his talents at the courthouse, the State house, and the White House. He may be a civil servant or a Senator, a candidate or a campaign worker, a winner, or a loser. But he must be a participant and not a spectator."

"Efforts and courage are not enough without purpose and direction. "

. JFK said it in a speech at the Coliseum in

Raleigh, North Carolina, on September 17, 19601. He was talking about the need for America to move forward and not stand still in the face of history and challenges. He emphasized that effort and courage alone are not enough to achieve progress and success, but they must be guided by a clear purpose and direction. He also said that Americans are tired of standing still and do not intend to be left behind.

This quote has been widely used and cited by many people who share the same vision and values as Kennedy. It reflects his leadership style and his charisma that inspired many people to act. It also reminds us of the importance of having a purpose and direction in our lives, and not just relying on our efforts and courage. Without a purpose and direction, we may lose sight of our goals and waste our time and energy. Having a purpose and direction gives us motivation, focus, and meaning. It helps us to overcome obstacles and achieve our dreams.

"If not us, who? If not now, when

The phrase "If not us, who? If not now, when?" is often attributed to various sources, including the famous American civil rights leader, John F. Kennedy, and the Jewish religious leader, Rabbi Hillel the Elder. While its exact origin may be debated, the quote is generally used to convey a sense of urgency and responsibility. It encourages individuals to act and assume responsibility for addressing important issues or challenges. Essentially, it emphasizes that if we don't step up to tackle a problem or take on a particular task, then who will, and if we don't act now, when will we? This quote is often used to motivate people to become proactive and make a positive difference in the world,

"Change is the law of life. You must either make a problem or solve one. "

That is a very interesting quote. It seems to suggest that life is dynamic and requires constant adaptation and creativity. I did some research and found out that the quote is attributed to John F. Kennedy, the 35th president of the United States. He said it in a speech at the University of North Carolina in 1961. He was talking about the challenges and opportunities of the modern world, and how America needed to be prepared to face them.

"Leadership and learning are indispensable to each other. "

This is a famous quote by John F. Kennedy, the 35th president of the United States, who was assassinated in Dallas, Texas, on November 22, 1963. The quote was part of his prepared speech that he never got to deliver at the Trade Mart in Dallas. The quote expresses his belief that leadership and learning are mutually dependent and beneficial, and that both are necessary for the progress and prosperity of a nation and the world. He also warns against the dangers of ignorance and misinformation in foreign policy, and the need for rational and informed decision-making. He criticizes those who offer simplistic and unrealistic solutions to complex problems, and those who oppose change and innovation. He praises the role of research and education in advancing society and the economy, and he acknowledges the contributions of the Dallas Citizens Council and the Graduate Research Center. of the Southwest. The quote is widely cited and admired as a reflection of Kennedy's vision.

and wisdom, and his commitment to excellence and enlightenment.

"Mankind must put an end to war, or war will put an end to mankind. "

The quote "Mankind must put an end to war, or war will put an end to mankind" is often attributed to John F. Kennedy, the 35th President of the United States. He made this statement during a speech he delivered at the American University in Washington, D.C. on

June 10, 1963, during the height of the Cold War between the United States and the Soviet Union.

In this speech, President Kennedy called for peace and nuclear disarmament, emphasizing the need for diplomatic efforts to prevent the escalation of the arms race and the potential catastrophic consequences of a nuclear conflict. The quote reflects his belief that humanity's survival depends on its ability to avoid and resolve conflicts through peaceful means rather than resorting to war, especially in the nuclear age when the destructive power of weapons had reached unprecedented levels.

Kennedy's speech at American University is considered a significant moment in the history of the Cold War, as it signaled a shift toward a more conciliatory and diplomatic approach to resolving the tensions between the superpowers. It also highlighted the existential threat posed by nuclear weapons and the urgency of achieving peace.

CHAPTER 3

Sir Winston Leonard Spencer Churchill

Sir Winston Leonard Spencer Churchill

(30 November 1874 — 24 January 1965) was a British statesman, soldier, and writer who served as Prime Minister of the United Kingdom twice, from 1940 to 1945 during the Second World War, and again from 1951 to 1955. Apart from two years between 1922 and 1924, he was a Member of Parliament (MP) from 1900 to 1964 and represented a total of five constituencies. Ideologically an adherent to economic liberalism and imperialism, he was for most of his career a member of the Conservative Party, which he led from 1940 to 1955. He was a member of the Liberal Party from 1904 to 1924.

"Success is not final, failure is not fatal: It is the courage to continue that counts. "

Generally attributed to Winston Churchill, the former British prime minister. However, there are some other possible sources for this saying, such as a poet, a medical doctor, and a Budweiser campaign in the 1930s. The exact origin of this quote is unclear, but it seems to have become popular by the 1960s.

"You have enemies? Good. That means you 've stood up for something, sometime in your life. "

This is a quote that is often attributed to Winston Churchill, but there is no evidence that he ever said it. The original source of the quote is the French writer Victor Hugo, who wrote in his 1845 essay "Villemain": "Vous avez des ennemis? Pourquoi, c'est l'histoire de tout homme qui a fait une grande action ou créé une idée neuve. C'est la nuée qui bruit autour de tout ce qui brille. Il faut que la renommée ait des ennemis, comme il faut que la lumiére ait des moucherons. Ne vous en inquiétez pas; dédaignez. Gardez votre sérénité comme vous gardez votre vie claire."

In English, this translates to: "You have enemies? Why, it is the story of every man who has done a great deed or created a new idea. It is the cloud which thunders around everything that shines. Fame must have enemies, as light must have gnats. Do not bother yourself about it, disdain. Keep your mind serene as you keep your life clear."

The quote has been modernized and simplified over time, and it has been used by various people, such as U.S. Senator Jim Bunning and rapper Eminem, to express their defiance of criticism and opposition. The quote implies that having enemies is a sign of courage and conviction, and that one should not be deterred by them. However, some might argue that having enemies is not always a good thing, and that it depends on the cause and the context of the conflict.

"The best argument against democracy is a five-minute conversation with the average voter. "

This is a quote that is often attributed to Winston Churchill, but there is no definitive evidence that he said it. According to the International Churchill Society, this quote is one of the many "red herrings" that Churchill never uttered. The society also provides a possible origin of this quote, which is from a 1905 play by George Bernard Shaw called Major Barbara, where a character says: "I know your quiet, simple, refined, poetic people like Adolphus—quite content with the best of everything! "

The quote is a cynical remark that implies that democracy is flawed because the average voter is ignorant, uninformed, or irrational. It suggests that a five-minute conversation with such a voter would be enough to convince anyone that democracy is not a good system of government. However, this quote does not consider the benefits of democracy, such as freedom, equality, human rights, and accountability. It also ignores the fact that democracy is not a static system, but a dynamic one that can evolve and improve over time.

Some people may agree with this quote, while others may disagree. It depends on one's perspective, values, and experience. However, it is important to remember that this quote is not a factual statement, but an opinion that may or may not reflect reality. Therefore, it is not a valid argument against democracy, but a rhetorical device that can be challenged and debated.

"In war, resolution; in defeat, defiance; in victory, magnanimity. "

This phrase appears on the frontispiece of

Churchill's magnificent "History of the Second World War." It is an apt description of the character and foresight of three great leaders in three successive centuries of our modern history: George Washington in the 18th Century, Abraham Lincoln in the 19th Century and Winston S. Churchill in the Twentieth Century.

Each was born within a decade of the passing of his predecessor, and each held his predecessor in high regard for leadership, tenacity, and character. Each cast a long shadow for succeeding generations.

George Washington became the father of his

Country because he represented the Noble Democratic American, a strong-willed, skilled soldier who spoke softly and fought bravely. Abraham Lincoln kept the flame of Liberty burning brightly; he spoke decisively and gave voice to the principles of Freedom and Democracy. And Winston Churchill, the half American and all-British Bulldog, stood alone in opposition to perhaps the most vile and despotic regime to have ever threatened the freedoms of not just England but of all free people and the principles that we all hold dear.

"A pessimist sees the difficulty in every opportunity; an optimist sees the opportunity in every difficulty. "

This quote is often attributed to Sir Winston

Churchill, the former Prime Minister of the United Kingdom. It reflects the idea that people can have different perspectives on challenges and opportunities.

Pessimist: This type of person tends to focus on the negative aspects of a situation. They see difficulties and obstacles as the primary elements and may be more inclined to avoid or give up on opportunities because they are daunted by the challenges involved.

Optimist: An optimist, on the other hand, has a more positive outlook. They see difficulties and obstacles as opportunities for growth and improvement. They are more likely to embrace challenges as a chance to learn, innovate, and achieve something meaningful.

This quote underscores the importance of having a positive mindset and being open to possibilities even in the face of adversity. It suggests that how we perceive, and approach challenges can significantly impact our ability to succeed and make the most of opportunities.

"To improve is to change; to be perfect is to change often. "

This is a famous quote attributed to Winston Churchill, the former Prime Minister of the United Kingdom. He said this in response to criticisms about the fact that he changed political parties. He meant that one should always be open to change and adapt to new circumstances, and that perfection is not a static state but a dynamic process. This quote can inspire us to embrace change as an opportunity for improvement and growth, rather than resist it or fear it.

"We shape our buildings; threequel, they shape us. "

This is a famous quote by Winston Churchill, the former Prime Minister of the United Kingdom. He said this during a debate about replacing the bombed-out House of Commons chamber in 19431. He wanted to rebuild it on the same spot and in the same style as the old one, even though it was too small for all the members of parliament. He believed that the shape and design of the building had an influence on the way the parliamentarians behaved and interacted. He argued that the intimate and adversarial layout of the chamber fostered a spirit of democracy and debate.

The quote has been used by many people to express the idea that architecture is not only a physical artifact, but also a social and cultural one. Buildings reflect the values and aspirations of the people who created them, and in turn, they affect the way the people who use them think and act. Buildings can inspire, challenge, comfort, or oppress us. They can also shape our sense of identity, community, and history.

"Courage is what it takes to stand up and speak; courage is also what it takes to sit down and listen. "

That is a very inspiring quote by Winston Churchill, who was the prime minister of the United Kingdom during World War Il. He was known for his leadership, eloquence, and courage in the face of adversity. He also won the Nobel Prize in Literature in 1953 for his speeches and writings.

The quote you shared means that courage is not only about speaking your mind and standing up for what you believe in, but also about listening to others and respecting their views. It takes courage to be open-minded and humble enough to learn from different perspectives. It also takes courage to admit when you are wrong or when you need to change your opinion.

I think this quote is very relevant for our times when there is so much polarization and conflict in the world. We need more courage to have civil and constructive dialogues with people who disagree with us, and to find common ground and solutions. We also need more courage to challenge ourselves and grow as individuals and as a society.

"If you 're going through hell, keep going. "

Seventy-two years ago tomorrow, a chubby, stoop-shouldered, funny faced man with a speech impediment took a new job. The man was 65-years old and until a year earlier was generally considered to be a crackpot and a political has-been. His taking the new job was one of the most momentous events of the entire 20th Century.

The man was Winston Churchill, and the job was Prime Minister of the United Kingdom. On May 10, 1940, the British looked to be finished. They stood alone against the vicious and victorious Nazis.

Two weeks after Churchill came into power,

France was knocked out of the war, and 340,000 British troops had to scramble to escape over the beaches at Dunkirk. The Germans had absolute control of all of Europe. It seemed impossible that Britain could survive.

With almost no hope left, the nation turned to Winston Churchill, the one man who had spoken the truth for years, saying nasty things about Adolf Hitler and the Nazis, even though it cost him in terms of political success and personal reputation.

"The price of greatness is responsibility. "

Effective leadership takes boldness. Without audacity, a will to win and a growth mindset, leadership is not sustainable.

I have watched some local companies defy the generational kiss of death by making brave decisions as the world around them changed. Leaders understand the importance of shifting paradigms to maintain relevance and real chances to win. I have seen new companies emerge, claiming their own unique position in the market and marching forward to future success. Leaders push themselves and those around them to reach for the unthinkable, the unspeakable and the unpredictable.

I have witnessed some communities across our nation make choices to rise above mediocrity and be known for something more than squeezing budgets in difficult economic times. Leaders acknowledge current realities and still push toward what is right.

I see individuals overcome significant obstacles, gaining hard-earned courage and leadership skills that drive them to do amazing things. Leaders don't let past challenges stand in the way of their future.

Leaders grow weary, but they press forward to cast vision and mobilize others to shape and achieve it. Our youth and region need vision casters who are willing to tackle tough issues and challenge our current comforts for our future prosperity.

Chapter 4

Abraham Lincoln

Abraham Lincoln, a self-taught lawyer, legislator, and vocal opponent of slavery, was elected 16th president of the United States in November 1860, shortly before the outbreak of the Civil War. Lincoln proved to be a shrewd military strategist and a savvy leader: His Emancipation Proclamation paved the way for slavery's abolition, while his Gettysburg Address stands as one of the most famous pieces of oratory in American history.

In April 1865, with the Union on the brink of victory, Abraham Lincoln was assassinated by Confederate sympathizer John Wilkes Booth. Lincoln's assassination made him a martyr to the cause of liberty, and he is widely regarded as one of the greatest presidents in U.S. history.

"Sir, my concern is not whether God is on our side; my greatest concern is to be on God's side, for God is always right. "

This is a quote attributed to Abraham Lincoln, the 16th president of the United States, who led the country during the Civil War. He reportedly said this in response to a minister who had praised the Union cause as being "the Lord's cause". Lincoln expressed his humility and reverence for God, and his desire to align himself with God's will, rather than assuming that God was on his side. This quote reflects Lincoln's deep faith and his recognition of the complexity and tragedy of the war. You can read more about this quote and its context in this article. How many legs does a dog have if you call the tail a leg? Four. Calling a tail a leg doesn't make it a leg. That is a clever riddle. It reminds me of a quote attributed to Abraham Lincoln, the 16th president of the United States. He reportedly said,

"How many legs does a dog have if you call the tail a leg? Four. Calling a tail, a leg doesn't make it a leg."

This quote is often used to illustrate the importance of logic and clear thinking. It also shows that words have meaning and cannot be changed arbitrarily. It is a sin to be silent when it is your duty to protest. This is a famous quote attributed to Abraham. Lincoln, the 16th president of the United States. He is said to have uttered these words in response to the injustice and oppression he witnessed in his country, especially regarding slavery and the Civil War. The quote expresses the moral obligation of speaking up against wrongdoings and defending the rights of others, even if it is risky or unpopular. The quote also implies that silence can be seen as a form of complicity or cowardice in the face of evil. The quote has been used by many activists and movements throughout history to inspire people to stand up for their causes and resist tyranny. One source that mentions this quote is an article titled "Daring to Speak, to Listen, and to Protest without Silencing" by Suzanne Nossel.

"If there is anything that links the human to the divine, it is the courage to stand by a principle when everybody else rejects it. "

Abraham Lincoln was known for his moral courage and his commitment to the principles of democracy and human rights. He led the nation through the Civil War, which was fought over the issue of slavery, and issued the Emancipation Proclamation, which freed the enslaved people in the Confederate states. He also delivered some of the most famous speeches in American history, such as the Gettysburg Address and the Second Inaugural Address. He was assassinated in 1865, shortly after the war ended.

The quote expresses Lincoln's belief that standing by one's convictions, even when they are unpopular or opposed by others, is a noble and divine act. He implies that such courage is a way of connecting with God, or a higher power, and that it is a rare and admirable quality. He also suggests that following the crowd or compromising one's principles is a sign of weakness or cowardice. Lincoln himself faced many challenges and criticisms during his presidency, but he remained steadfast in his vision of preserving the Union and ending slavery. He was willing to risk his life and reputation for what he believed was right.

The quote is inspiring and relevant for anyone who faces opposition or resistance to their beliefs or values. It encourages us to be brave and faithful to our ideals, and to not give up or give in to pressure or fear. It also reminds us that we are not alone in our struggles, and that we can find strength and guidance from a higher source. It challenges us to be true to ourselves and to our conscience, and to act with integrity and dignity.

"In times like the present, men should utter nothing for which they would not willingly be responsible through time and eternity. "

Abraham Lincoln said these words in his annual message to Congress on December 1, 1862, during the Civil Warl. He was urging the lawmakers to support his plan for emancipation of the slaves, which he announced in the Emancipation Proclamation on January 1, 1863. He wanted them to realize the gravity and importance of their decision, and the consequences it would have for the future of the nation and humanity. He also wanted them to speak with honesty and integrity, and not be swayed by passion or prejudice. This quote reflects Lincoln's moral courage and vision, as well as his eloquence and wisdom.

"A house divided against itself cannot stand. "

Lincoln's remarks in Springfield depict the danger of slavery-based disunion, and it rallied Republicans across the North. Along with the Gettysburg Address and his second inaugural address, the speech became one of the best-known of his career. It begins with the following words, which became the best-known passage of the speech:

I believe this government cannot endure permanently half slave and half free.

I do not expect the Union to be dissolved — I do not expect the house to fall — but I do expect it will cease to be divided It will become all one thing or all the other.

Either the opponents of slavery will arrest the further spread of it and place it where the public mind shall rest in the belief that it is in the course of ultimate extinction; or its advocates will push it forward, till it shall become lawful in all the States, old as well as new — North as well as South.

"I am a firm believer in the people, if given the truth, they can be depended upon to meet any national crisis. The great point is to bring them the real facts. "

The great point is to bring them the real facts," is often attributed to Abraham Lincoln, the 16th President of the United States. This quote underscores Lincoln's belief in the importance of honesty, transparency, and trust in government. He believed that when people are provided with accurate information and the truth, they can be relied upon to come together and address any national crisis effectively. This philosophy reflects the democratic principle of informed citizenry and the idea that an open and truthful government is essential for a healthy and functioning democracy.

"A nation that does not honor its heroes will not long endure. "

The quote, "A nation that does not honor its heroes will not long endure," is often attributed to Abraham Lincoln, the 16th President of the United States. However, there is some debate about its exact origin, and it's possible that the wording has evolved over time.

The essence of the quote conveys the importance of recognizing and honoring the contributions of individuals who have played significant roles in a nation's history or in the defense of its values and principles. This recognition is seen to foster a sense of unity, pride, and continuity within the nation, and to inspire future generations to continue the work of those who came before them.

Regardless of its precise origin, the sentiment behind the quote underscores the idea that a nation's ability to endure and thrive is closely tied to its ability to remember and appreciate its heroes and their contributions.

"Violence begins where knowledge ends. "

Emphasizes the idea that ignorance and a lack of understanding can contribute to conflicts and violence. When people lack knowledge, understanding, or the capacity to resolve disputes through peaceful means, they may resort to violence as a way to address their grievances or differences.

This quote underscores the importance of education, communication, and diplomacy in preventing conflicts and promoting peaceful coexistence. It suggests that a well-informed and educated society is more likely to find non-violent solutions to its problems and conflicts.

While the exact origin of this quote is unclear, it reflects a common theme in discussions about peace and conflict resolution, highlighting the role of knowledge and understanding in preventing violence.

"Character is like a tree and reputation like a shadow. The shadow is what we think of it; the tree is the real thing. "

This quote conveys a meaningful message about the distinction between a person's true character and the way they are perceived by others.

In this metaphor, "character" represents a person's moral and ethical qualities, their inner values, and their true nature. It is compared to a tree, which is a solid, enduring, and intrinsic part of a person.

On the other hand, "reputation" is likened to a shadow, which is fleeting and can change based on the angle of light or perspective. Reputation is how others perceive or think of a person based on their actions, behavior, and interactions with others.

The quote underscores the idea that while reputation can be influenced by external factors, rumors, or misperceptions, a person's true character remains constant and is the "real thing." It suggests that individuals should focus on building and maintaining their character, which is within their control, rather than obsessing over their reputation, which can be subject to external influences. In essence, it encourages authenticity and integrity in one's actions and values.

"History is not history unless it is the truth. "

Underscores the fundamental principle that the field of history should be based on accurate and factual information. History is the study of past events, and its primary goal is to understand and interpret the past as objectively and truthfully as possible.

Historians strive to uncover and present historical events, people, and circumstances based on credible evidence and reliable sources. While interpretations of history can vary, the core foundation of historical study is the pursuit of truth and the avoidance of bias, distortion, or manipulation of facts.

In essence, this quote emphasizes that for something to be considered "history," it must adhere to the principles of honesty, accuracy, and a commitment to discovering and presenting the truth about past events. It serves as a reminder of the importance of

rigorous research, critical analysis, and integrity in the study and documentation of history.

"Kindness is the only service that will stand the storm of life and not wash out. "

It suggests that acts of kindness have a lasting impact on individuals and communities, even in the face of adversity and life's challenges.

While many other aspects of life may be temporary or fleeting, the positive effects of kindness can endure. Kindness has the power to create connections, build trust, and leave a lasting impression on people's hearts and minds. In times of difficulty or hardship, acts of kindness can provide comfort, support, and a sense of hope.

This quote serves as a reminder of the profound and lasting significance of being kind to others and highlights the idea that kindness can be a source of strength and stability, both for individuals and for society.

"Tell the truth and you won 't have so much to remember. "

emphasizes the simplicity and practicality of honesty. It suggests that when you consistently tell the truth and are transparent in your words and actions, you don't have to keep track of lies or fabrications, which can be mentally and emotionally taxing.

This quote also highlights the ethical and moral value of honesty. Being truthful is not only easier to maintain but also contributes to trustworthiness and integrity in your relationships with others. When you tell the truth, you establish a reputation for credibility and reliability.

In essence, this quote encourages individuals to prioritize honesty as a fundamental principle in their interactions and communications, not only for the sake of simplicity but also for the sake of building and maintaining trust and integrity in their personal and professional lives.

.

CHAPTER 5

Martin Luther King Jr.

(January 15, 1929 — April 4, 1968) was a prominent American civil rights leader and activist who is best known for his role in advancing civil rights through nonviolent civil disobedience and advocacy for racial equality. He played a pivotal role in the American civil rights movement during the mid-20th century and is remembered for his inspirational speeches and peaceful protests. Here are some key aspects of Martin Luther King Jr.'s life and work:

Early Life and Education: Martin Luther King

Jr. was born in Atlanta, Georgia, to Reverend

Martin Luther King Sr. and Alberta Williams King. He grew up in a deeply religious and middle-class family. He attended segregated schools and graduated from Morehouse College with a degree in sociology. He later earned a doctorate in systematic theology from Boston University.

Montgomery Bus Boycott: King's involvement in the civil rights movement began with the Montgomery Bus Boycott in 1955. The boycott was a year-long protest racial segregation on public buses in Montgomery, Alabama, and it marked one of the first major successes of the civil rights movement. King's leadership during this boycott catapulted him into a prominent role in the movement.

Southern Christian Leadership Conference (SCLC): In 1957, King, along with other civil rights leaders, founded the Southern Christian Leadership Conference (SCLC). This organization was dedicated to achieving civil rights through nonviolent protest and civil disobedience.

March on Washington: On August 28, 1963,
Martin Luther King Jr. delivered his famous

"I Have a Dream"

speech during the March on Washington for Jobs and Freedom. This speech is one of the most iconic moments in American history and called for an end to racism and segregation.

Civil Rights Act of 1964: King's leadership and the efforts of the civil rights movement played a significant role in the passage of the Civil Rights Act of 1964, which outlawed discrimination based on race, color, religion, sex, or national origin. This was a major legislative milestone in the fight for civil rights.

Selma to Montgomery March: In 1965, King and other civil rights activists organized a series of marches from Selma to Montgomery, Alabama, to demand the right to vote for African Americans. The first march, known as "Bloody Sunday," was met with violence from law enforcement, but the subsequent marches led to the passage of the Voting Rights Act of 1965.

Nobel Peace Prize: In 1964, Martin Luther King Jr. was awarded the Nobel Peace Prize for his nonviolent struggle against racial inequality and his commitment to civil rights.

Assassination: Tragically, Martin Luther King
Jr. was assassinated on April 4, 1968, in Memphis, Tennessee. His death sparked outrage and grief across the nation and led to widespread mourning.

Legacy: Martin Luther King Jr.'s legacy is enduring. He is remembered as a symbol of nonviolent resistance, civil rights, and social justice. Martin Luther King Jr. Day, observed on the third Monday in January, commemorates his birthday, and celebrates his contributions to the fight for civil rights.

Continuing Influence: King's ideas and strategies for achieving social justice and equality continue to inspire activists and leaders around the world. His message of nonviolent protest and his vision for a more just and equitable society remain powerful and relevant.

Martin Luther King Jr. is one of the most iconic figures in American history, and his contributions to the civil rights movement have left an indelible mark on the United States and the world.

"Darkness cannot drive out darkness; only light can do that. Hate cannot drive out hate; only love can do that. "

Absolutely, the quote "Darkness cannot drive out darkness; only light can do that. Hate cannot drive out hate; only love can do that" is one of Martin Luther King Jr.'s most famous and powerful statements. It encapsulates his philosophy of nonviolence and the idea that positive change and justice can only be achieved through love, understanding, and peaceful means. This quote continues to resonate with people around the world and serves as a reminder of the enduring power of love and compassion in the face of adversity and hatred.

"Injustice anywhere is a threat to justice everywhere. "

It emphasizes the interconnectedness of justice and injustice, highlighting that when injustice is allowed to persist in one place, it poses a threat to justice everywhere. This quote underscores the idea that individuals and societies should not turn a blind eye to injustice, even if it does not directly affect them, as it ultimately erodes the foundations of a just and equitable society.

Martin Luther King Jr. used this quote to articulate the importance of solidarity and collective action in the struggle for civil rights and social justice. It serves as a reminder that addressing injustice is a moral imperative that transcends geographic and social boundaries, and it continues to inspire people to advocate for justice and equality in various contexts around the world.

"I have a dream that my four little children will one day live in a nation where they will not be judged by the color of their skin but by the content of their character, "

Martin Luther King Jr.'s famous "I Have a Dream" speech. Delivered during the March on Washington for Jobs and Freedom on August 28, 1963, this quote encapsulates King's vision for a future in which racial discrimination and prejudice would no longer define individuals' opportunities and worth.

In this powerful statement, King expresses his hope that future generations would experience a more just and equitable society, where people are evaluated based on their character and actions rather than the color of their skin. This quote continues to resonate with people worldwide and remains a symbol of the ongoing struggle for racial equality and civil rights. It serves as a reminder of the enduring importance of addressing racial discrimination and working toward a more inclusive and harmonious society.

"Our lives begin to end the day we become silent about things that matter. "

Is a poignant reminder of the importance of speaking out against injustice and acting on issues that are significant to us. Martin Luther King Jr. used this quote to emphasize the idea that remaining silent in the face of important moral and social issues is akin to surrendering one's life to complacency and apathy,

This statement underscores the notion that individuals have a responsibility to stand up for what they believe is right and just, even when it is difficult or uncomfortable. It serves as a call to action, encouraging people to use their voices and engage in activism to address the pressing problems of their time. King's message reminds us that positive change often requires courage, advocacy, and a commitment to making the world a better place for all.

"Freedom is never voluntarily given by the oppressor; it must be demanded by the oppressed. "

Reflects the idea that those who hold power and control are unlikely to grant freedom, rights, or justice to marginalized or oppressed groups without pressure and demands for change. Martin Luther King Jr. articulated this concept to underscore the importance of activism and the need for oppressed individuals and communities to assert their rights and advocate for their own liberation.

This quote emphasizes the agency and determination of those who are subjected to injustice and oppression. It implies that social progress often requires organized efforts, protests, and movements aimed at demanding equality and justice. King's words serve as a reminder of the role that grassroots activism and advocacy play in challenging systemic oppression and driving positive change in society.

"The ultimate measure of a man is not where he stands in moments of comfort and convenience, but where he stands at times of challenge and controversy. "

The quote "The ultimate measure of a man is not where he stands in moments of comfort and convenience, but where he stands at times of challenge and controversy" underscores the importance of character and integrity during difficult and morally complex situations. Martin Luther King Jr. used this quote to emphasize that a person's true character is revealed when they face adversity, adversity, and ethical dilemmas.

This statement encourages individuals to reflect on their actions and choices during times of hardship and controversy. It suggests that how a person behaves when facing challenges and standing up for their beliefs is a more accurate gauge of their moral and ethical fiber than how they conduct themselves during moments of ease and comfort.

Ultimately, this quote serves as a call to prioritize principles, justice, and doing what is right, even when it is difficult or unpopular. It has resonated with individuals striving for social change and ethical leadership, highlighting the importance of courage and conviction in the face of adversity.

"The time is always right to do what is right, "

The quote is a concise and powerful statement by Martin Luther King Jr. that encapsulates the idea that one should not wait for the perfect moment to take a stand for what is just and moral. Instead, it emphasizes the importance of acting with integrity and doing what is right at every opportunity, regardless of external circumstances.

This quote encourages individuals to be proactive in their commitment to justice, equality, and ethical conduct. It underscores the notion that one should not delay acting in the face of injustice or wrongdoing but should rather act with a sense of urgency and a commitment to what is right.

Martin Luther King Jr.'s message with this quote is that the responsibility to make the world a better place rests with everyone, and it is always the right time to stand up for what is just and moral. It has inspired countless individuals to act and advocate for positive change in their communities and beyond.

"We must accept finite disappointment, but never lose infinite hope.

Reflects belief in the enduring power of hope and resilience even in the face of setbacks and adversity. This quote encourages individuals to acknowledge and accept that disappointments and challenges are a part of life, but it also reminds them not to lose faith in the possibility of a better future.

King's words highlight the importance of maintaining a positive and hopeful outlook, especially when working toward long-term social change and justice. It suggests that setbacks and disappointments may be temporary, but the hope for a more just and equitable world should remain unwavering.

This quote has resonated with people seeking to overcome obstacles and continue their efforts in the face of adversity. It serves as a source of inspiration for those who work toward social justice, reminding them that hope can be a driving force for positive change even in difficult times.

"Nonviolence is a powerful and just weapon, which cuts without wounding and ennobles the man who wields it. It is a sword that heals. "

The quote by Martin Luther King Jr. eloquently expresses his philosophy of nonviolent resistance to achieve social change and justice.

In this statement, King portrays nonviolence as a potent tool for effecting change. He argues that nonviolence allows individuals and movements to challenge injustice and oppression without causing physical harm or perpetuating cycles of violence. Instead of inflicting wounds, nonviolence seeks to heal divisions and promote understanding.

Moreover, King suggests that nonviolence not only brings about external change but also elevates the moral character of those who practice it. It is a means by which individuals can demonstrate their commitment to justice, equality, and peace.

This quote remains a central tenet of King's legacy and continues to inspire activists and advocates for civil rights, social justice, and peace worldwide. It emphasizes the profound impact that nonviolent action can have in advancing the cause of justice while maintaining a commitment to empathy and healing.

"In the end, we will remember not the words of our enemies, but the silence of our friends. "

Highlights the importance of speaking out against injustice and oppression. It underscores the idea that remaining silent in the face of wrongdoing, discrimination, or injustice is a form of complicity.

King's words serve as a reminder that true friends and allies are those who stand up for what is right and just, even when it is uncomfortable or challenging. They refuse to be bystanders and instead use their voices and actions to support those who are marginalized or oppressed.

This quote also emphasizes the role that individuals and communities play in advocating for social change. It suggests that collective action and solidarity are essential in the struggle for justice and equality.

Ultimately, this quote encourages people to be vocal and active in the pursuit of a more equitable and just society, reminding us that our actions and voices have the power to make a difference and leave a lasting impact.
remaining silent in the face of wrongdoing, discrimination, or injustice is a form of complicity.

King's words serve as a reminder that true friends and allies are those who stand up for what is right and just, even when it is uncomfortable or challenging. They refuse to be bystanders and instead use their voices and actions to support those who are marginalized or oppressed.

This quote also emphasizes the role that individuals and communities play in advocating for social change. It suggests that collective action and solidarity are essential in the struggle for justice and equality.

Ultimately, this quote encourages people to be vocal and active in the pursuit of a more equitable and just society, reminding us that our actions and voices have the power to make a difference and leave a lasting impact.

Chapter 6

Nelson Mandela

Nelson Mandela was a South African anti-apartheid revolutionary, political leader, and philanthropist who served as President of South Africa from 1994 to 1999. He is widely regarded as one of the most significant figures in the 20th century for his role in ending apartheid, the oppressive system of racial segregation and discrimination enforced by the South African government.

Here are some key points about Nelson Mandela's life and legacy:

Early Life: Nelson Rolihlahla Mandela was born on July 18, 1918, in the village of Mvezo in Umtata, then part of South Africa's Cape Province. He belonged to the Thembu royal family.

Anti-Apartheid Activism: Mandela became involved in anti-apartheid activism in his youth and joined the African National Congress (ANC), a political organization that opposed apartheid policies.

Imprisonment: In 1962, Mandela was arrested and subsequently

sentenced to life imprisonment in 1964 for his involvement in planning sabotage against the apartheid government. He spent 27 years in prison, mostly on Robben Island.
Release and Negotiations: Mandela was released from prison on February 11, 1990, as South Africa began to transition away from apartheid. He played a crucial role in negotiations to dismantle apartheid and establish multiracial elections.
Presidency: In 1994, South Africa held its first democratic elections, and Nelson Mandela was elected as the country's first black president. His presidency was marked by efforts to reconcile the deeply divided nation and implement policies aimed at addressing the legacy of apartheid.
Truth and Reconciliation: Mandela supported the Truth and Reconciliation Commission, which aimed to bring healing and justice by allowing victims and perpetrators of human rights abuses to come forward and share their stories.
Retirement and Philanthropy: After leaving the presidency, Mandela continued to work on various humanitarian causes, including education and HIV/AIDS awareness through the Nelson Mandela Foundation.
Global Icon: Mandela became an international symbol of resistance to oppression, peace, and reconciliation. He received numerous awards and honors, including the Nobel Peace Prize in 1993.
Death: Nelson Mandela passed away on December 5, 2013, at the age of 95. His death was met with an outpouring of grief and tributes from around the world.
Nelson Mandela's life and legacy serve as a powerful example of the capacity for forgiveness, reconciliation, and the struggle for justice and equality. He is often referred to by his Xhosa clan's name, "Madiba," as a sign of respect and affection. His work laid the foundation for a more inclusive and democratic South Africa and inspired people worldwide in the fight against injustice and inequality.

"It always seems impossible until it's done. "

This powerful statement reflects the idea that many challenges and goals may appear insurmountable or impossible at first glance, but with determination, effort, and perseverance, they can be accomplished. It underscores the importance of believing in oneself and one’s abilities, even when faced with seemingly overwhelming obstacles. Ultimately, it encourages people to push through their doubts and fears to achieve their aspirations.

“The greatest glory in living lies not in never falling, but in rising every time we fall. “

This quote emphasizes the idea that success is not defined by avoiding failure altogether but by one's ability to bounce back and overcome adversity when faced with challenges or setbacks. It underscores the resilience and determination required to achieve greatness in life. Instead of being discouraged by failures, it encourages individuals to view them as opportunities for growth and learning, ultimately leading to greater achievements.

"For to befree is not merely to cast off one's chains, but to live in a way that respects and enhances the freedom of others. "

This quote encapsulates the deeper meaning of freedom. It suggests that true freedom is not just about breaking free from one's own constraints and limitations but also about using that freedom responsibly and in a way that doesn't infringe upon the freedom and rights of others. It underscores the importance of living in a just and equitable society where individual freedom is balanced with the respect for the freedom and rights of others, promoting a harmonious and fair coexistence.

"I learned that courage was not the absence of fear, but the triumph over it. The brave man is not he who does not feel afraid, but he who conquers that fear. "

This quote beautifully captures the essence of courage by highlighting that being brave doesn't mean never experiencing fear but rather facing and overcoming that fear. It emphasizes that true courage lies in one's ability to confront and conquer their fears, demonstrating resilience and determination in the face of adversity. It encourages individuals to act despite their fears and anxieties, and in doing so, they can achieve remarkable things.

"No one is born hating another person because of the color of his skin, or his background, or his religion, People must learn to hate, and if they can learn to hate, they can be taught to love, for love comes more naturally to the human heart than its opposite. "

Nelson Mandela's autobiography, "Long Walk to Freedom." This powerful statement speaks to the idea that hatred and prejudice are learned behaviors and not inherent in human nature. It underscores the potential for positive change and the capacity for love and empathy that exists within each person. Mandela's message is one of hope and the belief that through education and understanding, it is possible to overcome prejudice and foster a more inclusive and harmonious society.

"Education is the most powerful weapon which you can use to change the world. "

This emphasizes the transformative power of education. It suggests that knowledge, learning, and education are essential tools for bringing about positive change and progress in the world. Education can empower individuals to make informed decisions, challenge injustice, and contribute to the betterment of society. Mandela's words highlight the idea that investing in education is not only an investment in personal growth but also a means to create a more just and equitable world for everyone.

"A good head and a good heart are always a formidable combination. "

This statement underscores the idea that when intelligence and rational thinking (a good head) are coupled with empathy, compassion, and moral values (a good heart), an individual becomes a powerful force for positive change and leadership. It suggests that a balanced and harmonious integration of intellectual and emotional qualities can lead to effective and ethical decision-making, which is especially important in leadership roles and in addressing complex issues in the world.

“I dream of an Africa which is at peace with itself. “

This statement reflects his vision and aspiration for a unified and peaceful continent. Nelson Mandela, a prominent figure in the struggle against apartheid in South Africa and later the President of South Africa, was known for his commitment to reconciliation and unity. This quote emphasizes his hope for an Africa where internal conflicts, divisions, and tensions are resolved, and nations can coexist in harmony and cooperation. It's a vision of Africa's future where peace prevails, and people from diverse backgrounds can live together in peace and prosperity.

"It is in your hands to create a better world for all who live in it. "

This powerful statement emphasizes the individual and collective responsibility we all must contribute to positive change and the betterment of society. It underscores the idea that we can all play a role in making the world a more just, compassionate, and equitable place through our actions, choices, and efforts. This quote serves as a call to action,

"Our human compassion binds us the one to the other—not in pity or patronizingly, but as human beings who have learnt how to turn our common suffering into hope for the future. "

Reflects the idea that compassion is a unifying force among people. It suggests that rather than feeling pity or condescension, true compassion connects individuals on a fundamental human level. When people share in the experiences of suffering and hardship, they can come together in empathy and solidarity, using their collective strength to find hope and create a better future. This quote underscores the power of compassion to foster unity and resilience in the face of adversity.

Chapter 7

Mahatma Gandhi

Mahatma Gandhi,
whose full name was Mohandas Karamchand Gandhi, was a prominent Indian leader and a key figure in the Indian independence movement against British colonial rule. He is widely regarded as a symbol of nonviolent resistance and civil disobedience. Here are some key aspects of Gandhi's life and his contributions:

Early Life: Mohandas Karamchand Gandhi was born on October 2, 1869, in Porbandar, a coastal town in present-day Gujarat, India. He came from a devout Hindu family and later embraced principles from various religious traditions.
South Africa: Gandhi initially studied law in London and then went to South Africa to work as a lawyer. It was in South Africa where he

first became involved in civil rights activism, fighting against racial discrimination and injustice faced by the Indian community. there. His experiences in South Africa profoundly influenced his approach to activism and nonviolent resistance.

Nonviolent Resistance: Gandhi is best known for his philosophy of nonviolence, which he called "Satyagraha." He believed in the power of nonviolent civil disobedience to bring about social and political change. His famous salt march, or Dandi March, in 1930, in protest of the British salt tax, is a prime example of his nonviolent resistance.

Indian Independence Movement: Gandhi returned to India in 1915 and quickly became a leader in the Indian National Congress, which was at the forefront of the movement for India's independence from British colonial rule. His methods of peaceful protest, fasting, and noncooperation inspired millions of Indians to join the struggle for freedom.

Salt March: One of Gandhi's most iconic acts of civil disobedience was the Salt March, a 240-mile journey to the Arabian Sea where he and his followers made salt from seawater in defiance of the British salt monopoly. This campaign had a significant impact on India's independence movement.

Role in Negotiations: Gandhi played a pivotal role in negotiating with the British authorities for India's independence. His efforts culminated in the declaration of India's independence on August 15, 1947.

Assassination: Tragically, Mahatma Gandhi was assassinated on January 30, 1948, in New Delhi by a Hindu nationalist who disagreed with his views on nonviolence and religious tolerance.

Legacy: Gandhi's philosophy of nonviolence and civil disobedience had a profound influence on other civil rights movements around the world, including the American civil rights movement led by Martin Luther King Jr. His teachings on truth, love, and justice continue to inspire people globally in their struggle for social justice and human rights.

Mahatma Gandhi is remembered as the "Father of the Nation" in India for his tireless efforts in leading the country to independence through peaceful means. His life and work continue to serve as a source of inspiration for those advocating for justice, equality, and human rights.

"You must be the change you want to see in the world. "

It underscores the idea that personal transformation and in dividual actions are essential for creating a better and more just world. Gandhi's message here is a call to take responsibility for one's beliefs and values and to live them in daily life. By embodying the principles and changes we wish to see in society, we can inspire others and contribute to broader social and political change. This quote continues to be a powerful reminder of the importance of personal agency in making the world a better place.

"An eye for an eye only ends up making the whole world blind. "

This statement conveys Gandhi's profound belief in nonviolence and the futility of revenge or retaliation. He argued that seeking revenge only perpetuates a cycle of violence and harm, ultimately harming everyone involved. Instead, he advocated for resolving conflicts and seeking justice through peaceful means and reconciliation. This quote serves as a reminder of the destructive nature of revenge and the importance of seeking peaceful solutions to conflicts.

"The best way to find yourself is to lose yourself the service of others. "

This quote emphasizes the idea that one's true purpose and fulfillment can often be discovered through selfless service and helping others. When individuals devote themselves to the well-being and service of their communities and fellow human beings, they often gain a deeper understanding of themselves and their values. It underscores the notion that self-discovery and personal growth are intertwined with acts of kindness, compassion, and service to others.

"The weak can never forgive. Forgiveness is the attribute of the strong. "

In this quote, Gandhi suggests that forgiveness is not a sign of weakness but rather a demonstration of strength. It takes strength and inner resilience to let go of anger, resentment, and the desire for revenge in favor of forgiveness and reconciliation. Gandhi believed that forgiveness was a powerful force for healing and reconciliation, and he practiced it in his philosophy of nonviolent resistance. This quote encourages individuals to embrace forgiveness as a way to resolve conflicts and promote peace and understanding.

"In a gentle way, you can shake the world. "

This quote conveys the idea that even small, peaceful, and compassionate actions can have a profound and transformative impact on the world. Gandhi himself was a proponent of nonviolent resistance, and he believed that positive change could be achieved through nonviolent means.
This quote encourages individuals to recognize the power they possess to make a difference in the world, not through force or aggression, but through gentleness, kindness, and a commitment to justice and truth. It reminds us that each person has the potential to contribute to positive change and create a better world through their actions and choices.

"First they ignore you, then they laugh at you, then they fight you, then you win. "

This describes the typical progression of how a new or unconventional idea or movement is initially met with indifference, then ridicule, opposition, and ultimately success. Gandhi's own life and his leadership in the Indian independence movement are often cited as an example of this pattern.
The quote encourages perseverance and resilience in the face of adversity, suggesting that those who stay committed to their cause and principles can ultimately achieve their goals, even when faced with initial skepticism and opposition. It has been used as a source of inspiration for various social and political movements around the world.

"You can chain me, you can torture me, you can even destroy this body, but you will never imprison my mind. "

Reflects the indomitable spirit and commitment to freedom and justice often associated with Mahatma Gandhi. While Gandhi

himself faced various forms of persecution and imprisonment during his struggle for Indian independence and his advocacy for nonviolent resistance, this quote encapsulates his belief that the human spirit and the quest for truth and justice cannot be suppressed or imprisoned.
It conveys the idea that physical suffering and oppression can never extinguish the inner resolve and determination to stand up for one's beliefs and principles. Gandhi's message in this quote serves as a powerful reminder of the resilience of the human spirit and the enduring power of ideas and ideals even in the face of adversity.

"Freedom is not worth having if it does not include the freedom to make mistakes. "

Is a thought-provoking quote that underscores the importance of individual liberty and the acceptance of human imperfection. It suggests that true freedom encompasses the ability to make choices, even if those choices lead to errors or mistakes.
This quote encourages a society that values individual autonomy and recognizes that people should have the freedom to learn and grow from their experiences, even when those experiences involve making mistakes. It emphasizes the idea that freedom should not be overly constrained by fear of making errors, as the process of making mistakes and learning from them is an integral part of personal and societal progress.

"The greatness of a nation and its moral progress can be judged by the way its animals are treated. "

This underscores the idea that a society's treatment of animals reflects its moral character and ethical values. It suggests that a compassionate and humane approach to animals is indicative of a society's overall moral and ethical development.
Gandhi's message here advocates for the fair and ethical treatment of all living beings, emphasizing the interconnectedness of all life. It encourages people to consider their responsibilities toward animals and to strive for a society that respects and protects the well-being of animals as a measure of their moral greatness and progress. This quote has been influential in the animal rights and welfare movements.

"Civilization is the encouragement of differences. "

The idea that the progress of a society or civilization is often linked to its ability to embrace and celebrate diversity. While the origin of this quote is not commonly attributed to Mahatma Gandhi, the sentiment aligns with his philosophy of nonviolence, tolerance, and inclusivity.

The quote suggests that a truly civilized society values and encourages differences among its members, whether those differences are related to culture, beliefs, ethnicity, or other aspects of identity. It implies that rather than seeking to homogenize or suppress differences, a civilization that thrives is one that recognizes the richness and strength that diversity brings. This concept has become an important element of discussions on social harmony and progress in our globalized world.

These quotes reflect Gandhi's philosophy of nonviolence, his emphasis on personal responsibility and service to others, and his commitment to justice and social progress. His words continue to inspire and resonate with people around the world.

Chapter 8

Albert Einstein

Albert Einstein (March 14, 1879 — April 18, 1955) was a German-born physicist who is widely regarded as one of the most influential scientists of the 20th century. His groundbreaking work in theoretical physics, particularly his theory of relativity, revolutionized our understanding of the fundamental laws governing the universe.

Here are some key points about Albert Einstein's life and contributions:

Theory of Relativity: Einstein's theory of relativity, including the special theory of relativity (published in 1905) and the general theory of relativity (published in 1915), fundamentally changed our understanding of space, time, and gravity. His famous equation, $E=mc^2$, demonstrated the equivalence of mass and energy.

Nobel Prize: In 1921, Einstein was awarded the Nobel Prize in Physics for his explanation of the photoelectric effect, which is a crucial component of quantum mechanics.
Emigration to the United States: Einstein emigrated to the United States in 1933, escaping Nazi Germany and settling in Princeton, New Jersey. He accepted a position at the Institute for Advanced Study.
Humanitarian and Political Activism: Einstein was an advocate for civil rights, pacifism, and nuclear disarmament. He was a vocal critic of nuclear weapons and played a role in the establishment of the Bulletin of the Atomic Scientists.
$E=mc^2$: His equation, $E=mc^2$, represents one of the most famous equations in physics and is often used to describe the relationship between energy (E), mass (m), and the speed of light (c).
Thought Experiments: Einstein was known for his thought experiments, which he used to explore complex physical concepts. The most famous of these is perhaps the "twin paradox," which is used to illustrate the effects of time dilation in special relativity.
Photoelectric Effect: His work on the photoelectric effect helped establish the concept of quantization in the behavior of light and paved the way for the development of quantum mechanics.
Unified Field Theory: Einstein spent much of his later career working on a unified field theory, attempting to reconcile electromagnetism and gravity into a single framework. He was not successful in achieving this goal.
Legacy: Albert Einstein's contributions to science have left an indelible mark on our understanding of the physical world. His theories continue to be tested and validated through experiments, and they have practical applications in fields such as GPS technology and the study of the cosmos.
Death: Einstein passed away on April 18, 1955, at the age of 76. His brain was preserved for scientific study, and researchers continue to investigate various aspects of his life and work.
Einstein's name is synonymous with genius, and his work continues to inspire scientists, philosophers, and thinkers across the world. His insights into the nature of the universe and the importance of intellectual curiosity have had a lasting impact on human knowledge and exploration.

"The world will not be destroyed by those who do evil, but by those who watch them without doing anything. "

Powerful quotes are often attributed to Albert Einstein. This statement underscores the importance of acting and standing up against injustice, oppression, and wrongdoing. It suggests that passive bystanders who do nothing in the face of evil can contribute to the perpetuation of harm and the deterioration of the world's moral fabric.
This quote serves as a reminder of the collective responsibility we must speak out and take action against injustice and cruelty, as complacency and inaction can have dire consequences. It emphasizes the role of individuals in shaping the world's destiny through their choices and actions.

"Imagination is more important than knowledge. For knowledge is limited, whereas imagination embraces the entire world, stimulating progress, giving birth to evolution. "

It reflects his perspective on the significance of imagination in the context of knowledge and progress. Let's break down the quote:

"Imagination is more important than knowledge."

: Einstein suggests that imagination holds a higher value or importance than knowledge. While knowledge is essential, he emphasizes that imagination surpasses it in certain aspects.

"For knowledge is limited":

Einstein acknowledges that knowledge has its limitations. Knowledge is the accumulation of facts, information, and understanding that we gain through learning and experience. However, it is finite and can only encompass what we currently know.

"Imagination embraces the entire world."

: Imagination, according to Einstein, has the power to extend beyond the boundaries of existing knowledge. It allows us to explore possibilities, scenarios, and ideas that go beyond the constraints of what is currently known or understood.

"Stimulating progress, giving birth to evolution":

Einstein implies that imagination is a catalyst for progress and evolution. It is through creative and imaginative thinking that new ideas, inventions, and innovations emerge. These, in turn, lead to advancements in science, technology, and society.
In essence, Einstein's quote highlights the complementary relationship between knowledge and imagination. While knowledge provides the foundation upon which progress is built, imagination expands the boundaries of what is possible and drives innovation. Both are essential in the pursuit of understanding and growth, but imagination plays a crucial role in pushing the boundaries of human achievement.

"The only thing that interferes with my learning is my education. "

It reflects his perspective on the potential limitations of formal education. Let us explore its meaning:

"The only thing that interferes with my learning is my education."
"Interferes with my learning."

: Einstein suggests that something is getting in the way of his ability to learn or acquire knowledge. In this context, he is referring to an obstacle or hindrance.

"My education":

Here, "education" refers to the formal, structured process of learning that takes place in schools, colleges, and universities. It involves curriculum, rules, and established methods of teaching.

Einstein's quote implies that sometimes, the formal education system itself can hinder or limit a person's ability to learn. It suggests that there may be aspects of traditional education that do not align with an individual's preferred learning style, interests, or creative thinking. This quote highlights the idea that true learning can occur beyond the boundaries of formal education, and one should not be confined by the limitations of a structured system.

Einstein himself was known for his unconventional thinking and ability to question established norms, which may have contributed to his perspective on the potential interference of education with learning. Nonetheless, it's essential to recognize that education can also be a valuable tool for acquiring knowledge and skills, and it serves as a foundation upon which individuals can build their understanding of the world.

"The release of atomic energy has not created a new problem. It has merely made more urgent the necessity of solving an existing one. "

Albert Einstein, and it reflects his perspective on the release of atomic energy and its implications. Let's break down the meaning of the quote:

"The release of atomic energy has not created a new problem."

Einstein is referring to the development of atomic energy, particularly in the context of the atomic bomb and nuclear technology. He suggests that the release of atomic energy, while groundbreaking and significant, did not introduce a completely new problem to humanity.

"It has merely made more urgent the necessity of solving an existing one."

In this part of the quote, Einstein emphasizes that the existence of atomic energy has heightened the urgency of addressing a preexisting problem or challenge. The "existing problem" he alludes to is likely the potential for destructive warfare and the need to prevent the devastating consequences of nuclear conflict.

Einstein's quote underscores the idea that the discovery and use of atomic energy come with great responsibilities. It amplifies the need for international cooperation and diplomacy to prevent the misuse of such powerful and destructive technology. In essence, he is urging humanity to confront the ethical, moral, and geopolitical challenges posed by atomic energy and to work towards its responsible and peaceful use.

Nationalism is an infantile disease. It is the measles of mankind. "

Reflects his perspective on nationalism. Let's break down the meaning of the quote:

"Nationalism is an infantile disease. "

Einstein characterizes nationalism as an "infantile disease." By this, he means that nationalism is akin to a childish or immature outlook or behavior. He may be suggesting that nationalism can be driven by simplistic and narrow-minded thinking, often rooted in a strong attachment to one's own nation or ethnicity at the expense of a broader and more nuanced worldview.

"It is the measles of mankind. "

By comparing nationalism to measles, Einstein is using a metaphor to emphasize his point. Measles is a contagious and potentially harmful disease that spreads easily. Einstein likens nationalism to this disease to convey the idea that it can spread throughout humanity, causing divisions, conflicts, and harm in its wake.
In essence, Einstein's quote expresses his concern about the negative consequences of extreme nationalism, which can lead to divisiveness, xenophobia, and conflict on a global scale. He advocates for a more cosmopolitan and cooperative perspective that transcends narrow nationalistic interests in pursuit of peace and understanding among all people.

"Peace cannot be kept by force; it can only be achieved by understanding. "

It emphasizes the importance of understanding and diplomacy in achieving and maintaining peace. Let's break down its meaning:

"Peace cannot be kept by force."

: This part of the quote suggests that using force, coercion, or aggression is not an effective means of achieving long-lasting peace. Attempting to impose peace through military action or oppressive measures may lead to temporary calm, but it is unlikely to result in a sustainable and just peace.

"It can only be achieved by understanding."

: Here, Einstein emphasizes that true and enduring peace can only be attained through understanding. Understanding implies empathy, open communication, cooperation, and a willingness to resolve conflicts through dialogue and negotiation. It involves acknowledging and respecting the perspectives, needs, and rights of all parties involved.
In essence, Einstein's quote underscores the idea that peace is a product of human relationships and cooperation, not dominance or control. It suggests that to create a peaceful world, people and nations must seek to understand one another, find common ground, and work together to address conflicts and challenges. This quote aligns with the principles of diplomacy, conflict resolution, and international cooperation as essential tools in the pursuit of global peace.

"The world is a dangerous place to live; not because of the people who are evil, but because of the people who don't do anything about it. "

The quote you provided highlights the idea that the world can be a dangerous place due to the inaction of individuals in the face of evil or wrongdoing. While the origin of this quote is not definitively attributed to one particular person, it reflects a sentiment often expressed by those concerned with issues of injustice and moral responsibility.
Here's a breakdown of the quote's meaning:

"The world is a dangerous place to live."

: This part of the quote acknowledges that there are inherent dangers and risks in the world, which can include various forms of injustice, violence, and wrongdoing.

"Not because of the people who are evil."

: The quote distinguishes between the inherent dangers of the world and the people who intentionally engage in evil actions. It suggests that evil people, while a concern, are not the primary source of danger in the world.

"But because of the people who don't do anything about it"

: The quote's main message lies here. It points out that a significant source of danger in the world comes from those who witness or are aware of evil actions but choose to do nothing to address or rectify them. This inaction, often driven by indifference, apathy, or fear, can allow injustice and wrongdoing to persist and even escalate.
In essence, this quote underscores the importance of acting against injustice and evil. It suggests that a lack of action, whether due to complacency or inaction, can contribute to a world where harmful actions go unchecked. It encourages individuals to stand up against injustice, work toward positive change, and take responsibility for making the world a safer and more just place.

"The measure of intelligence is the ability to change. "

The quote you provided emphasizes that intelligence is not solely about knowledge or innate abilities but is closely linked to the capacity to adapt and change. While the exact origin of this quote is not definitively attributed to a single individual, it aligns with the broader idea that intelligence is dynamic and involves the following key points:
Intelligence as Adaptability: The quote suggests that one's intelligence can be measured by their ability to adapt and evolve in response to new information, challenges, and changing circumstances. In other words, intelligence is not fixed but flexible.
Openness to Learning: It implies that intelligent individuals are open

to new ideas, willing to reevaluate their beliefs, and eager to learn and grow. They do not rigidly adhere to old ways of thinking but are receptive to change.

Problem-Solving: Intelligence often involves problem-solving skills. Intelligent individuals can analyze situations, identify potential solutions, and make informed decisions, which often require the ability to change one's approach when necessary.

Life-Long Learning: The quote also suggests that intelligence is a lifelong pursuit. It's not something one achieves and then stops. Instead, it involves ongoing curiosity and a willingness to adapt and improve over time.

In summary, this quote emphasizes that intelligence goes beyond mere knowledge and encompasses the ability to change, adapt, and grow intellectually and personally. It encourages individuals to embrace change and view it as an opportunity for learning and improvement, recognizing that the capacity to change is a fundamental aspect of human intelligence.

"In the middle of every difficulty lies opportunity. "

This conveys the idea that even in challenging or adverse situations, there is the potential for positive outcomes and opportunities for growth. Here is a breakdown of its meaning:

"In the middle of every difficulty":

This part acknowledges the presence of difficulties, problems, or obstacles in life. It suggests that challenges are an inherent part of the human experience and are often encountered in various aspects of life.

"Lies opportunity":

The quote asserts that within these difficulties, there are hidden or untapped opportunities waiting to be discovered. It implies that challenges can serve as a catalyst for personal and professional development.

In essence, this quote encourages a positive and proactive mindset when facing difficulties. It prompts individuals to seek out and recognize the potential benefits, lessons, or chances for improvement that can emerge from challenging situations. It underscores the idea that adversity can be a steppingstone to personal growth and success, provided one approaches it with resilience and an open mind.

"It's not that I'm so smart; it's just that I stay with problems longer, "

Einstein's perspective on problem-solving and the importance of persistence and determination in the face of challenges. Here's a breakdown of its meaning:

"It's not that I'm so smart":

Einstein humbly downplays his own intelligence, suggesting that his success is not solely attributed to exceptional intelligence or innate talent. He acknowledges that being "smart" is not the only factor at play.

"It's just that I stay with problems longer."

: The key to Einstein's problem-solving prowess, according to the quote, is his willingness to engage with problems persistently and tenaciously. He does not give up easily but instead continues to work on problems until he finds a solution or gains a deeper understanding.

In essence, this quote highlights the importance of perseverance, patience, and resilience when confronting challenges. It emphasizes that success often comes from putting in the effort and dedicating time and energy to solving problems rather than relying solely on one's innate intelligence. It encourages others to adopt a similar mindset of persistence in their own pursuits.

These quotes reflect Einstein's wisdom and insight into issues of social justice, peace, and the human condition, demonstrating that his intellect extended beyond the realm of science to address broader societal concerns.

Chapter 9

George Orwell

George Orwell, pseudonym of Eric Arthur
Blair, (born June 25, 1903, Motihari, Bengal, India— died January 21, 1950, London, England), English novelist, essayist, and critic famous for his novels.
Animal Farm (1945) and Nineteen Eighty-four (1949), the latter a profound anti-utopian novel that examines the dangers of totalitarian rule.
Born Eric Arthur Blair, Orwell never entirely abandoned his original name, but his first book, Down and Out in Paris and London, appeared in 1933 as the work of George Orwell (the surname he derived from the beautiful River Orwell in East Anglia). In time his nom de plume became so closely attached to him that few people, but relatives knew his real name was Blair. The change in name corresponded to a profound shift in Orwell's lifestyle, in which he changed from a pillar of the British imperial establishment into a

literary and political rebel.

"Big Brother is watching you. "

The phrase refers to the government's surveillance of the people with listening devices and cameras, in a totalitarian society, where Big Brother is the head of the totalitarian regime. Everyone in this society is under surveillance by the authorities, which reminds people of an endless catchphrase "Big Brother is watching You," showing a dictator's mindset of a Big Brother. The idea conveys a line of propaganda, meaning citizens must follow what a dictatorial government wants them to do, and if they do not, Big Brother will know, as it spies on them all the time.

"He who controls the past controls the future. He who controls the present controls the Past. "

In "1984," the dystopian superstate of Oceania is run by the fictional English Socialist Party, known in the Newspeak language of Oceania as Ingsoc. Ingsoc is led by a mysterious (and mythical) leader known only as "Big Brother." The protagonist of the novel is.
Winston Smith, a member of the middle class known as the "Outer Party" who lives in London, the capital city in Oceania. The year is 1984 (Orwell was writing in 1949), and Winston, like everyone else in the novel, is under the thumb of the charismatic Big Brother's totalitarian government.
Winston is an editor in the Records.
Department at the governmental office Ministry of Truth, where he actively revises historical records to make the past conform to whatever Ingsoc wants it to be. One day he wakes up and thinks, Who controls the past, controls the future: who controls the present, controls the past... The mutability of the past is the central tenet of Ingsoc. Past events, it is argued, have no objective existence, but survive only in written records and in human memories. The past is whatever the records and the memories agree upon. And since the Party is in full control of all records, and in equally full control of the minds of its members, it follows that the past is whatever the Party chooses to make it.

"We shall meet in the place where there is no darkness. "

"We shall meet in the place where there is no darkness" is a phrase attributed to O'Brien, a member of the Inner Party, in the novel "1984" by George Orwell. Winston dreams of O'Brien saying these words to him, and later realizes the reference is to the Ministry of Love, where the lights are always on and where Winston is taken to be tortured. The phrase is also interpreted as a symbol of hope for a future where people are free to think and behave as they please.

"In a time of deceit telling the truth is a revolutionary act. "

The quote "In a time of deceit telling the truth is a revolutionary act" is often attributed to George Orwell, but there is no evidence that he said it. The quote is a variation of a quote by Arthur Conan Doyle, which reads "In a time of universal deceit - telling the truth is a revolutionary act". The quote suggests that telling the truth is a revolutionary act in times of deceit and that all truth passes through three stages: ridicule, violent opposition, and acceptance as being self-evident.

"The further a society drifts from truth the more it will hate those who speak it. "

This quote is often attributed to George Orwell, but it is a misattribution. The earliest version of this quote that we could find came from a 2009 column by the conservative writer Selwyn Duke, on the right-leaning website RenewAmerica.com. The quote reads, "The further a society drifts from Truth, the more it will hate those who speak it".

"Men can only be happy when they do not assume that the object of life is happiness. "

This is a reflection on the idea that happiness is not something that can be pursued directly. Rather, it is a byproduct of living a meaningful life and pursuing worthwhile goals. When we focus too much on our own happiness, we may become less happy eventually.

Instead, we should focus on living a life that is fulfilling and meaningful, and happiness will naturally follow.
"Sanity is not statistical. "

From the novel 1984 by George Orwell. It is spoken by the protagonist, Winston Smith, and is a reflection on the idea that sanity is not something that can be determined by the majority. In the novel, the government uses propaganda and manipulation to control the thoughts and actions of its citizens. Winston's statement is a reminder that even if everyone around you believes something to be true, it doesn't necessarily make it so. Sanity is not determined by the majority, but by the individual's ability to think critically and independently.

"Journalism is printing what someone else does not want printed: everything else is public relations. "

A reflection on the idea that journalism should be about uncovering the truth and exposing things that people or organizations would rather keep hidden. In contrast, public relations are about shaping and controlling the narrative to present a positive image of a person or organization. In other words, journalism should be about holding people accountable and speaking truth to power, while public relations is about protecting and promoting the interests of those in power.

Chapter 10

John Emerich Edward Dalberg-Acton, 1st Baron Acton

(1834-1902), commonly known as Lord Acton, was an English Catholic historian, politician, and writer. He is best known for his embark,

"Power tends to corrupt, and absolute power corrupts absolutely".

Acton was a strong advocate of individual liberty and believed that political liberty was essential to the preservation of religious liberty. He was also a prolific scholar and historian and made the history of liberty his life's work.

"Power tends to corrupt, and absolute power corrupts absolutely. "

That is a famous quotation by Lord Acton, a
19th century British politician and historian.
He wrote it in a letter to Bishop Mandell Creighton in 1887, expressing his view that people who have too much power tend to abuse it and become morally corrupted. He also said that "great men are almost always bad men" when they have absolute authority.
The idea that power corrupts is not new. It can be traced back to ancient times, such as the writings of Plato and Aristotle, who

warned of the dangers of tyranny and despotism. In the modern era, many other writers and thinkers have expressed similar sentiments, using different words. For example, William Pitt the Elder, a British prime minister in the 18th century, said that "unlimited power is apt to corrupt the minds of those who possess it" in a speech to the House of Lords in 1770. Alphonse de Lamartine, a French poet, and politician in the 19th century, wrote that "absolute power demoralizes" and that "it is not only the slave or serf who is ameliorated in becoming free. The master himself did not gain less in every point of view, for absolute power corrupts the best natures" in an essay published in 1848.

The quotation by Lord Acton is often used as a proverb or a warning to remind people of the potential negative effects of having too much power. It is also sometimes used as a criticism or an explanation for the actions of certain historical figures or political leaders who have been accused of being corrupt or tyrannical. Some examples are Roman emperors,
Napoleon Bonaparte, Adolf Hitler, Joseph
Stalin, Mao Zedong, and Saddam Hussein. However, the quotation is not meant to be taken as an absolute or universal truth. There may be exceptions or counterexamples of people who have wielded great power without becoming corrupt or evil. Some possible candidates are Abraham Lincoln, Winston Churchill, Mahatma Gandhi, Nelson Mandela, and Dalai Lama.

"The one pervading evil of democracy is the tyranny of the majority, or rather of that party, not always the majority, that succeeds, by force or fraud, in carrying elections, "
It is often paraphrased as **"Power tends to corrupt, and absolute power corrupts absolutely".**

The phrase "tyranny of the majority" refers to a situation in which most of an electorate pursues exclusively its own objectives at the expense of those of the minority factions. This results in oppression of minority groups comparable to that of a tyrant or despot, as argued by John Stuart Mill in his 1859 book "On Liberty". The concept of tyranny of the majority is an inherent weakness to majority rule, in which most of an electorate pursues exclusively its own objectives at the expense of those of the minority factions.

In a democratic system, it is important to ensure that the rights of the minority are protected and that the majority does not abuse its power. This can be achieved through various mechanisms such as constitutional limits on the powers of a legislative body, the introduction of a Bill of Rights, and a separation of powers.

"Liberty is not the power of doing what we like, but the right of being able to do what we ought. "

Attributed to Lord Acton, a British historian and politician. The word "liberty" has several meanings, but in this context, it refers to the state of being free from oppressive restrictions imposed by authority on one's way of life, behavior, or political views.
Lord Acton's quote emphasizes that liberty is not the power of doing what we like, but the right of being able to do what we ought to do. It implies that liberty comes with responsibility and that we should use our freedom to do what is right and just.

"Despotic power is always accompanied by corruption of morality. "

The quote is often paraphrased as "Power tends to corrupt, and absolute power corrupts absolutely".
The quote suggests that when people have too much power, they are likely to become corrupt and lose their moral compass. This is because they are not held accountable for their actions and can act with impunity. Despotic power, which is characterized by absolute authority and control, is particularly prone to corruption of morality. The quote is still relevant today, as we see many examples of people in positions of power who have become corrupt and lost their moral compass. It is important to hold people accountable for their actions and to ensure that power is not concentrated in the hands of a few.

"A wise person does at once, what a fool does at last. Both do the same thing; only at different times. "

A wise quote! It reminds me of the saying, "Procrastination is the thief of time." The difference between a wise person and a fool is that the former understands the value of time and acts accordingly, while the latter does not. The wise person knows that time is a finite resource that cannot be regained once it is lost, so they make the most of it. The fool, on the other hand, squanders their time and only realizes its value when it's too late. It's always better to act sooner rather than later, especially when it comes to important matters. Thank you for sharing this quote with me!

"Men cannot be made good by the state, but they can easily be made bad. Morality depends on liberty. "

The quote suggests that the state cannot make people good, but it can certainly make them bad. It implies that morality is not something that can be imposed from the outside, but rather something that comes from within. According to Acton, morality depends on liberty, which means that people must be free to make their own choices and live their lives as they see fit. When people are free, they are more likely to act in accordance with their own moral principles, rather than being forced to follow the dictates of the state. This is because freedom allows people to think for themselves and to act on their own conscience, rather than being coerced into doing what the state wants them to do. In other words, liberty is a necessary condition for morality to flourish.

"When you perceive a truth, look for the balancing truth. "

This quote suggests that when we perceive a truth, we should also look for the balancing truth. It implies that there are often multiple perspectives to consider and that we should strive to see things from different angles. By seeking out the balancing truth, we can gain a more complete understanding of the situation and make more informed decisions. This approach can be especially useful when dealing with complex issues or when trying to resolve conflicts. Rather than simply accepting one point of view, we can explore different perspectives and find common ground.

"History is not a burden on the memory but an illumination of the soul. "

This quote is attributed to John Dalberg Acton, a British historian and politician who lived in the 19th century. According to him, history is not a burden on the memory but an illumination of the soul 1. This quote suggests that history is not just a collection of facts and figures, but rather a source of inspiration and enlightenment. By studying history, we can gain a deeper understanding of the world around us and the people who came before us. We can learn from their triumphs and mistakes and use this knowledge to make better decisions in the present. History can also help us appreciate the richness and diversity of human experience and inspire us to strive for a better future.

"Limitation is essential to authority. A government is legitimate only if it is effectively limited. "

This quote is attributed to the political philosopher Edmund Burke. The idea of limited government is a key concept in the history of liberalism and political philosophy. A government that is limited in power is considered legitimate, as it is effectively controlled and can exercise control. The concept of limited government is closely associated with constitutions. The United States Constitution of 1789 and the French Constitution of 1793 were both enacted to reaffirm limited government, although in different ways. The U.S. Constitution achieved limited government through a separation of powers: "horizontal" separation of powers distributed power among branches of government (the legislature, the executive, and the judiciary, each of which provide a check on the powers of the other); "vertical" separation of powers (federalism) divided power between the federal government and the state government. James Madison, one of the authors of the Federalist Papers, noted that the Framers of the American Constitution sought to create a government that was capable of both being controlled and of exercising control. Madison wrote in Federalist No. 51 that "the great security against a gradual concentration of the several powers in the same department, consists in giving to those who administer each department, the necessary constitutional means, and personal motives, to resist encroachments of the others" 1. The idea of limited government has been influential in political philosophy and has been used to justify various political positions, including libertarianism and classical liberalism.

"It is easier to find people fit to govern themselves than people fit to govern others. "

The quote suggests that it is easier to find people who can govern themselves than it is to find people who are capable of governing others. This is because people who can govern themselves are more likely to be self-aware, responsible, and accountable for their actions. On the other hand, people who are capable of governing others may be more prone to corruption, abuse of power, and authoritarianism.

THE END

www.ingramcontent.com/pod-product-compliance
Ingram Content Group UK Ltd.
Pitfield, Milton Keynes, MK11 3LW, UK
UKHW021829270726
14058UKWH00001B/53

9 798330 323371